FEED THE CHILDREN FIRST

IRISH MEMORIES of the GREAT HUNGER

FEED THE CHILDREN FIRST

IRISH MEMORIES of the GREAT HUNGER

Edited by Mary E. Lyons

Atheneum Books for Young Readers

NEW YORK · LONDON · TORONTO · SYDNEY · SINGAPORE

To my brother, Joseph Lyons
Go dtéigh tú slán í gcónaí
Go safely, always

Atheneum Books for Young Readers
An imprint of Simon & Schuster Children's Publishing Division
1230 Avenue of the Americas
New York, New York 10020
Text copyright © 2002 by Mary E. Lyons
Book design by Becky Terhune
The text of this book is set in Caslon Antique.
Printed in Hong Kong
2 4 6 8 10 9 7 5 3 1
Library of Congress Cataloging-in-Publication Data
Feed the children first: Irish memories of the Great Hunger / edited by Mary E. Lyons—1st ed.
p. cm.
Includes bibliographical references.
ISBN 0-689-84226-0
1. Ireland—History—Famine, 1845-1852—Juvenile literature. [1. Ireland—History—Famine, 1845-1852.] I. Lyons, Mary E.
DA950.7 .F45 2002

941.5081—dc21   00-049606

FIRST
EDITION

Contents

Sketch of child in Galway

The Great Hunger
1845–1852

I heard me aunt say it was nothing to see a woman with six or seven children come into a house that time looking for a bite to eat, and the woman of the house would give her a noggin of milk and stirabout made of oaten meal. She would feed the children first, then herself, and on to the next house.   —*Kate Flood, County Longford*

———

The great hunger is hard to imagine. Photographs help us understand the horrors of American slavery and the Jewish Holocaust. Yet no photograph of Ireland's worst famine is known to exist, though pictures taken during later Irish famines show similar conditions. Several Irish newspapermen made sketches when they traveled through the stricken country in 1847. Later, Irish painters told parts of the story on canvas. These are our only images of what the Irish remember as the "hard times."

The story of the great hunger begins with a lumpy potato and ends with a puzzle. In 1845, over eight million people lived in Ireland. Smaller than our state of North Carolina, the island was a colony of England. Most Irish rented squares of land (some as small as one-quarter of an acre) from absentee landlords who lived in England. Here they grew potatoes—an easy crop to raise in the wet Irish weather. A knobby type known as the "lumper" grew best.

If a farmer didn't pay his rent, the landlord's agent could force him and his family off the land. So farmers also grew oats, barley, wheat, cabbage, carrots, and turnips. After harvest, most of the crops were sold to pay the landlord's twice-yearly fee.

Potatoes, then, were all that were left for the Irish people to eat. A family with four children consumed about five tons a year! The potato is a plain-looking food, yet it is rich in protein and vitamin C. With oat bread, buttermilk, and an occasional piece of fish or rabbit, Irish families managed to survive.

In the summer and fall of 1845, a plant fungus spread throughout Ireland. The lumper potato was hit especially hard. This was not the first time disease had struck the potato crop in Ireland, but it was the worst. When entire fields of potato stalks rotted, people began to starve. Some managed to save a few seed potatoes. These they planted the next year.

Then, unbelievably, the fungus attacked again in 1846. During the cold, snowy winter of 1847, millions of Irish lay sick or dying from hunger and fever. Those who lived on the coast were too weak even to catch fish. This year of death lives in Irish memory as Black '47. In 1848, the death rate was higher still.

The worst of the famine was over by 1852. By then, one million Irish men, women, and children were dead. Another 1.5 million had fled by boat. Exiled by hunger, most of them came to the United States. They were searching, quite literally, for scraps of food to keep themselves alive.

The great Irish famine was one of the worst disasters of the nineteenth century. Why did it happen? The question still puzzles people today.

Beginning with King Henry VIII in the 1500s, England had ruled Ireland with a cruel hand. English Protestants despised Irish Catholics, so the government seized Irish land and gave it to English landlords. In 1695, the government passed laws forbidding Irish people to buy land, hold office, attend school, speak the Irish language, or worship as Catholics.

The last of the strict laws ended in 1829, but the damage was done. Many Irish lived in great poverty on land they did not own. The poorest could not read or write. This gave the English an excuse to look down on their island neighbors. To them, the Irish were a different and backward race, though only thirteen miles of water separated the two bodies of land. Some historians think this racism made it easy for the English to watch the Irish starve.

After the great hunger began, English businessmen continued to buy wheat, corn, meal, and flour grown on Irish farms owned by landlords. As Irish-grown food left the country, the English government bought Indian corn from America and shipped it to Ireland. Sometimes the export and import ships even passed one another. What's worse, food coming into Ireland was not given freely to the people. Men, women, and children were forced to work on "relief" projects in exchange for it. As more people died, soup kitchens were set up for a short while.

In 1847 the English government began to withdraw its help. Now landlords and local Irish officials, they said, must provide the food. It was as if the English thought the Irish deserved to suffer. "God brought the blight," one Irishman said, "but the English brought the famine."

Fortunately, the Society of Friends (Quakers) donated food, cash, clothes, and bedding in the early years of the famine. Later they gave farmers free seeds. A group of English businessmen called the British Relief Association helped, too. The money they raised in America and England paid for broth and rye bread. The food kept thousands in the west of Ireland, especially schoolchildren, alive. Two of these children were my great-grandfather and great-grandmother, who were nine and six years old when the great hunger began.

A number of Irish people still detest the landlords for their part in the famine. Some landlords fed their tenants and let them stay on the land. The worst ones forced families to leave their cottages at gunpoint when they couldn't pay the rent. Evictions continued after the great hunger, as did periodic famine.

Between 1879 and 1894, the same fungus struck the potato crops nine more times. During these years and into the twentieth century, another six million people poured out of Ireland. They were seeking a better life, and most found it. Now over forty million Irish descendants live in the United States. You may be one of them.

The Irish who died in the famine could leave no stories behind, and most who lived kept their terrible memories to themselves. Luckily in the 1940s, the Irish Folklore Commission asked children and grandchildren of survivors to remember stories passed down through their families. Some of these were published in 1995 in *Famine Echoes*, edited by Cathal Póirtéir.

Many of the accounts in *Feed the Children First* are abridged from Póirtéir's collection. A few are adapted from published writings by the Irish storytellers, J. M. Synge, Seumus McManus, and James Berry. Two reports are by Englishmen, and one is from a Scotsman. Otherwise, all the memories in this book are Irish.

Irish memories of the great hunger are painful to read, but they have much to teach us about today. From Haiti to Bangladesh, from Afghanistan to Africa, people are still hungry and malnourished. Children suffer most. According to Unicef, six million youngsters under the age of five in 1995 died from lack of nutritious food. The Irish famine is worth remembering when hunger organizations ask us to help them feed the children first.

For current information about hungry children, visit these World Wide Web sites:

Unicef: http://www.unicef.org
Share Our Strength: http://www.strength.org
International Famine Centre: http://www.ucc.ie/famine

Children dancing in the crossroads

The People

Owen and his wife, Sheila, owned a little one-room cabin in which they reared seven brave boys and girls. Owen was the rarest *shanachie* [storyteller] our lad ever listened to. He told stories as if with honey, and they flowed just as smooth.

Owen's story might begin: "Once upon a time when pigs were swine, when turkeys chewed tobacco, and pigeons built their nests in old men's beards—when every road in Ireland was paved with lovely pancakes, and little pigs with a knife and fork stuck in the back of each ran up and down the roads, crying, 'Come eat me! Come eat me!'"

And so the *shanachie's* great tale was off to a gorgeous start.

—*Seumus MacManus, County Donegal*

The blind piper

Down to the year of the Great Famine of 1846, a certain kind of social gathering was called a "Cake." It was something like a raffle. Supposing a poor family lost their only cow and had no earthly means of replacing her. The mother of the family went to some friendly publican [tavern keeper]. From him she got on credit five or ten gallons of whiskey, and some wine and cordials.

She then went to the baker. He baked her a great cake for the raffle—about two or three stone [about thirty to forty pounds] in weight. Next she engaged the services of a musician. This was easily done, for the pipes in those days were as plentiful as blackberries in autumn.

When the people of the surrounding villages heard about the cake raffle, they gathered at the house in hundreds. They were decked out in their best holiday attire. Peasant girls appeared in cashmere shawls and fine lace caps, which were garnished with nosegays and decorated with ribbons of various colours.

In front of the house was a little sloping lawn. In the center stood a churn, its handle driven firmly into the ground. A white homemade linen towel was spread over the top of the churn, on which was laid the great cake.

The custom was that whoever won the cake should call for a round of drinks for the whole gathering. Then the spree began in real earnest. When it was over, the woman was able to pay her creditors, and clear the price of a little cow as well.

The very last gathering of this kind was held in my native village on the Saint Patrick's Day before the famine. Although I was then only about six years old, I have a clear recollection of it, for it was held quite near the cabin in which I was born.

All the people were gathered in a vast crowd. The piper, a young blind man, sat on a chair in the open air. He was playing "Haste to the Wedding." It was a wonderful and glorious sight to see him seated and playing, sometimes sweeping the keys of his pipes with great, long fingers.   —*James Berry, County Mayo*

Connemara girl

Homespuns have been made in these mountain districts from time immemorial. In my childhood days, the peasantry made their own blankets and flannels. They made these in white and grey for home wear. Blue cloth was for men's wear.

There were also beautifully dyed goods made from lichen and other vegetable dyes. The people then made all their linens for sheets, towels, shirts. These happy times passed away with the famine years.

I was then a very small boy. After ten years away at school, I found a sad change on my return home. Many of the people were dead and gone. All who could emigrate fled, and those home industries fled with them. Almost all who remained bought cast-off clothing—the refuse of English and Scotch cities.   —*A Donegal man*

Connemara cottages

The Houses and the Land

The houses were low and thatched. Some had only one room divided from the kitchen by a thick stone wall. The better class of farmers had two rooms to their cottages besides the kitchen. Sometimes, in the back sidewall of the kitchen near the fire, a place for a bed was built out. The older people slept there for comfort and warmth. This spot was called the out-shot.

The floors were just earth. They stayed cold and damp during the long periods of rain in the wintertime. In times of deep snow, the clay became absolutely sticky by snow dragged in on the feet. The windows were small and often could not be opened to let in the fresh air. Missing panes sometimes did this to a certain degree.

—*William Torrens, County Donegal*

The population was very big before the Famine. It was three or four times thicker. There was a house on nearly every four acres of land around here. Some people had only two acres, and some had only one. . . .

If you cross Tierworker Mountain you will see where they set potatoes in ridges on it. The ridges are there still. You would wonder at anybody setting potatoes in such places where there is nothing but heather and long grass. But the place was so thickly populated that they had to plant potatoes there.

—*Barney Gargan, County Cavan*

Irish cabin with children outside

They lived from hand to mouth. Any failure in the crops meant great privation. Generally there was no money laid by. There was little money in circulation, and there was no food stored up in the event of crop failure.

The small farms were brought about by the father dividing a farm among two, three, or more sons. A son got married, and he built a house on a corner of the farm. He was given a few acres or a field or two to till. Another son got another patch. And so the original farms were carved up.

There weren't any new farms created unless the landlord thought he could increase his rental by doing so. Potatoes were the main food from August to Christmas for dinner, breakfast, and supper. —*J. O'Kane, County Sligo*

One of the first things that attracts the eye of a stranger in Ireland is the police he meets—on every road, in every village, even on the farmland, and on the seashore and the little islands that lie out in the sea.

These policemen wear a dark green uniform and are armed. This is what makes them remarkable—they have belts and pouches, ball cartridges in the pouches, short guns called "carbines," bayonets, pistols, and swords.

The next thing that struck me has been this—rent is usually paid through the sheriff and the armed police. The agent of the landlord is usually the buyer. He sends the corn, pigs, and potatoes to a seaport town for shipment to England. The landlord gets his rent by their sale in England.

It is no wonder that the Irish tenants were always poor and starving, or only kept from starving by a miserable diet of potatoes. While those who see the Irish corn, cattle, and pigs coming to England think the Irish are well-fed to have so much to spare. —*Alexander Somerville, a Scotsman*

The potato diggers

Potatoes and the Blight

The usual way of eating potatoes in the poor homes was out of a large basket made of unpeeled rods. After the potatoes were boiled, the pot was dumped into the basket on the doorstep and the water allowed to drain off. "Teeming the spuds," this was called. The potatoes were left in the basket, which was set down in the middle of the kitchen floor.

The people of the house then sat round in a circle on stools, with some salt on another stool near the basket, and noggins of buttermilk, which they balanced in their laps or set down on the earthen floor. No knives or forks were used.

The potatoes were boiled in their jackets and peeled with the left or right thumbnail. The nail was kept at a certain length for this purpose. So expert were the people at peeling potatoes that nobody with a knife and fork could take a potato jacket half as quickly.

If a large fish took the place of the buttermilk and salt, it was dumped in upon the potatoes in the basket. Everybody took a piece off with their fingers and thumb as the supper went on. Some had oaten meal for a few winter months.

—*William Torrens, County Donegal*

The discovery of the potato blight in Ireland

There have been three cruel plagues out through the country since I was born in the West. First, there was the big wind of 1839. That tore away the grass and green things from the earth.

Then there was the blight that came on the ninth of June in the year 1846. Up to then the potatoes were clean and good. But that morning a mist rose up out of the sea. You could hear a voice talking near a mile off across the stillness of the earth.

It was the same the next day, and the day after, and so on for three days or more. And then you could begin to see the tops of the stalks lying over as if the life was gone out of them. And that was the beginning of the great trouble and famine that destroyed Ireland.

Then God sent down the third plague. That was the sickness called the "choler" [cholera]. All the people left the town of Sligo—it's in Sligo I was reared—and you could walk through the streets at the noon of day and not see a person. You could knock at one door and another door and find no one to answer you. The people were traveling out north and south and east with the terror that was on them. The country people were digging ditches across the roads and driving people back, for they had great dread of the disease.
                                                                    —*An old man in County Wicklow*

Donkey carrying seaweed

Searching for Food

During the Famine, people on the coast used all the usual foods to be found along the shore: dulse [seaweed], sloak [algae], winkles [snails], barnacles, and cockles. Dulse is not edible until after the first severe frost in winter. It can be cooked immediately after being pulled. It has to be boiled for two or three hours.

—Sean Ó Beirne, County Donegal

They often went tramping for fluke, This meant going barefooted into the channel where these flatfish were plentiful. They put a foot down on the fish as they swam lazily around, then flung them high and dry up on the strand. Many dozens could be secured this way in a short time. *—William Torrens, County Donegal*

Launching the curragh

The coastal natives also captured and killed seabirds. They gathered eggs of seafowl in the lofty cliffs and rocks. From time to time, as weather permitted, men essayed forth in their hide "curraghs" [canoes] to the rock islands to capture and collect birds and eggs. Some were preferable to others as food. Yet all were accepted and none was rejected.

—*James Cormack, County Mayo*

Did you ever hear of blind herring? Well, blind herring was nothing more or less than salt and water. A little salt was added to water in a shallow vessel. The potatoes were dipped in it. Blind herring was "kitchen" [flavoring] for the potatoes when there was nothing else to be had.

—*J. O. Kane, County Sligo*

I heard my mother and others refer to an attack made on meal carts bringing English meal [Indian corn imported from America by the English government]. The carts were guarded by two soldiers and the drivers. The attackers had scythes fixed to handles like pikes. Others carried pitchforks. They were ordered to halt by the soldiers, but the attackers came on.

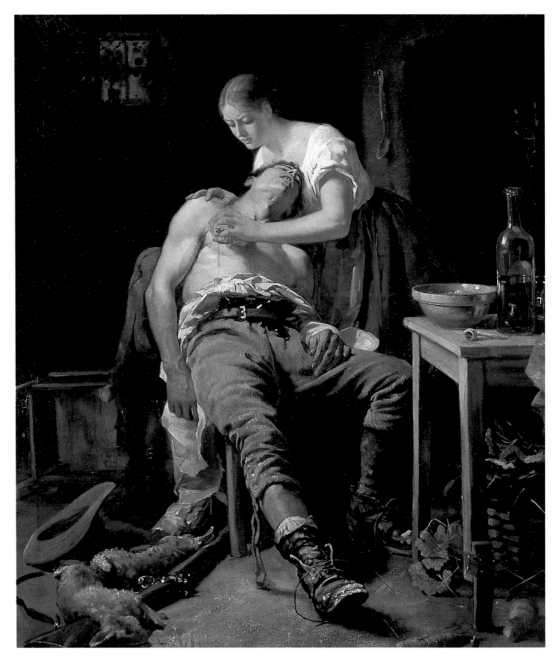

The Wounded Poacher

One solider took aim, and the other pretended to do so. . . . His bullet passed over the attackers' heads. The other wounded a poor fellow in the abdomen. The attackers promptly cut some of the bags of meal in two to make them more easy for quick transport. Then they cleared off. The poor, wounded chap was carried away but died later.

—*Pilib Ó Conaill, County Meath*

Garumna Island. Dinner of Indian meal, supplied by Relief Committee, 1898

I heard my father saying that the government didn't allow the Indian meal to come in until it was too late. . . . I heard my father saying how "generous" Queen Victoria [the Queen of England] was, that what relief she allowed would come to about a quarter of what was needed by the starving people. And the meal wouldn't firm—a mule couldn't leave the trace of her hoof on it. It would run a mile on a plank and scald a man the end of it!

———

Irish famine—interior of a hut

Some of the people were so desperate from starvation that they didn't wait for it [the meal] to be cooked properly. They ate it almost raw. That brought on intestine troubles. It killed a lot of them that otherwise might have survived. They just grabbed the meal and swallowed it down almost raw."

—*Peter Clarke, County Cavan*

Woman begging at Clonakilty

Starvation

We came to Clonakilty, where the coach stopped for breakfast. And here for the first time, the horrors of the poverty became visible in the vast numbers of famished poor. They flocked around the coach to beg for alms.

Amongst them was a woman carrying in her arms the corpse of a fine child. She was making the most distressed appeal to the passengers for aid to enable her to purchase a coffin and bury her dear little baby. I learned from the people of the hotel that each day brings dozens of such applicants into the towns.

—*James Mully, County Cork*

Perhaps the poor children presented the most piteous and heartrending spectacle. Many were too weak to stand. Their little legs were thin, except for frightful swellings. Every childish expression had entirely departed. In some, reason and intelligence had evidently flown.

Many were orphaned little relatives taken in by the equally homeless, and even by strangers. For these poor people are kind to one another to the end. They did but rarely complain. When we asked what was the matter, the answer was alike in all: "Indeed, the hunger."
                                    —*William Bennett, English Quaker , County Mayo*

Boy and Girl at Cahera

Sketch of child in Galway

My grandmother told me of her experience when a girl of seventeen in those awful days. Her people had a little country shop. She said it was not unusual to see corpses lying by the roadside with pieces of grass or leaves in their mouths. Their faces were stained with the juice of plants they were chewing to satisfy their hunger.

On one occasion a mother came with a baby in her arms. The poor little thing was gaunt. She kept whining for something to eat. The mother would persist in putting its lips to her breasts, which were milkless, in order to stop its crying. A drink of milk was given to the baby and its mother. Later the same day the mother was seen dead by the roadside with the baby still alive in her arms.

—*Felix Kernan, County Monaghan*

The poorhouses supplied coffins very cheap to any persons who were unable to purchase a coffin for their deceased friend. To be buried in a workhouse coffin was regarded as a slur on the friend and on the deceased.

So when a death occurred, friends of the deceased went to town for the "Burial Charge." They bought three boards, paint, and mounting. Some handyman made the coffin, and the coffin was carried to the grave on white linen sheets. A child's coffin was covered with white cloth instead of paint. —*Kathleen Hurley, County Galway*

Interior of a cabin. Carraroe, County Galway, 1898

Fever

The "Black Fever" followed. This appeared in black spots that gradually crossed the body. Lips became bloodless. Death followed in the home if they were not removed to the workhouse hospital. There seems to be no tradition that anyone catching the disease survived. *—Patrick Flannelly, County Mayo*

I mind Katchy Kerly saying they died with the cholera. They took it first, I mind her to say, between the two big toes, and it turned black and it went up the foot and the leg and into the body, and it turned as black as behind the fire till it killed them on their two feet in no time at all. *—Mary Nugent, County Armagh*

A woman from the Teelin district, on the death of her little son, was unable to get a coffin. She put the child in the cradle, strapped the cradle on her back and carried it five miles to the nearest graveyard, and buried it. Coffins of fever victims were always tarred on the inside. This was a precaution against any ooze and a sort of disinfectant.

—*Seán Mac Cuinneagáin, County Donegal*

There was a fever hospital and a cholera house. . . . Patients were removed to the cholera house when there was no hope of their recovery. In some cases the patients were dead on admittance. They were buried in bottomless coffins in a large pit in the corner of the present graveyard.

These coffins had hinges attached to the bottoms. A trigger was pulled, and the body was let drop into the pit. Some clay was filled in over the body, then lime was added. The corpse was buried without a habit, a sheet, or anything else available was wrapped around the body. Oftentimes this sheet or blanket was used again to cover a victim still living.

—*William Naddy, County Kilkenny*

The famine in Ireland—funeral at Skibbereen

At the gate of a workhouse

The Poorhouse

A very old man told me it was nothing strange to see people by the fences at the road-sides in a dying condition. They had left their homes and were looking for a bite to eat from anyone who could give it to them.

Some of them were strangers to the locality. They were not left on the roadside. Someone with a horse or donkey took the poor creatures to the poorhouse, where they did not live long.

One poor man took his mother to the poorhouse in a donkey and cart. On his way home he found two poor creatures by the roadside. He turned around and took them to the poorhouse also. Three journeys he made on that day and the last time he went, the place was so overcrowded that they were lying near the lane way to it.

—Seamus Reardon, County Cork

Little Liza Morrison

Old Mrs. Corcoran went into Granard Workhouse and took out three children. Their father and mother had died of the fever, and the children were brought away to the workhouse. Inside the green wall of the workhouse, a row of beds was inside the wall, and some thatch [straw] or something covering them. All the people in them beds had the fever, and it was believed that if you threw green fruit into each bed, you'd escape the fever.

And Mrs. Corcoran, she had a bag of green apples, and she went along the row of beds, one bed to other, looking for the children. And she threw a green apple into each bed she passed, to keep her from bringing home the disease with her. She got the children and brought them home with her. She had no child of her own.

But after a while some friends (that is, relatives) of the chidren came and took them away from her. They sent them to the United States to friends out there. And I often saw that old woman crying and telling that story. How the children were taken from her and sent to America, after she taking them from the workhouse.

—*Kate Flood, County Longford*

The central soup depot

Soup Kitchens

The rush to obtain a place for the distribution is surprising. Also surprising is the quiet demeanor of the poor people. To the present time, not an act of dishonesty has been known to take place. Not a spoon or vessel is missing.

The food is cooked in an upper building, then handed down for distribution. The upper gate is opened at twelve o'clock. Eight hundred are admitted. The tremendous rush presents fearful evidence of the hunger and misery that the crowd are enduring. The whole group are served in about three hours. They are then let out by the lower gate, and a fresh batch of five to six hundred is admitted as before.

—An English journalist in County Cork

Recipe for soup given to tenants on estate in County Limerick:

Quantity of water 190 quarts
Beef 30 pounds
Barley 8 pounds
Peas 8 pounds
Turnips 3 stone [about 42 pounds]
5 pennyworth of vegetables, leeks, greens, and celery, adding salt to taste

Accident on the relief works, Garumna Island, 1898. M. M'Donagh—age eighty—had his leg broken.

Relief Works

The people were very glad to get employment on these Public Works. They accepted it rather than take the free meal. The pay was ten pence a day for the common laboring man. The overseer, or "ganger," got two pence a day more.

The men worked in gangs digging out the hills. They removed stones and filled in the hollows. There would be six or eight men loosening the earth. Four would fill barrows with the stuff, and four would wheel. Two men worked at each barrow, and they took it in turns to shovel and wheel. They had to make a double run of twenty-four to thirty yards and back.

It was knacky work. A man had to be very careful. . . . The tip-head was the worst part. He had to run down along a nine-inch plank with his full barrow to the tip-head, tip out the stuff, and turn back. If he was not careful and knacky, he might topple his barrow over or maybe fall after it himself.

The "whip-up," as they called the overseer, watched the men all the time while he walked around cracking a whip. If a man showed any slackness or weakness at all, he was knocked off at once. There was always plenty of men waiting around to get work. There might be a hundred men sitting on the boundary to see if any man would drop out.

Some men had to walk four or five miles daily to their work, or even farther. The only rest during the day was the dinner hour. Before and after that it was backbreaking heavy labor all the time.   —*Bridget Keane, County Westmeath*

Relief works, Carraroe Island; women carrying stones, 1898

Women as well as men used to work on the road. They barrowed clay and stones. The women were paid one and a half pence a day. The men were paid two pence.... Every day, and sometimes several times a day, funerals used to pass—a couple of old people and children carrying naked remains covered with a bit of sacking on an old handbarrow.

The gaffer used to allow the squad of workers to carry the remains to the next squad, and so on as far as the workers went on the road. But the old people had to finish the journey on their own.   —*Liam Ó Briain, County Leitrim*

The ejectment

Eviction

My father said when one trouble was over they had to face another. The rent warners were out looking for two years' rent, but the people hadn't it. They sold everything they could sell. Some poor farmers sold even their last cow to pay something. Others couldn't pay anything.

The poor tenants didn't know what was going on, until one spring morning the town land was full of redcoat soldiers. From one end to the other, they put out every tenant in the town. My father often and often told how the redcoat soldier rode up on his horse to the door and asked for the man of the house.

"We want possession of this place," said the soldier. "You'd better clear out."

My father was like a man would be after getting a blow. He stood looking at the red-coat, unable to speak.

"Get to work and clear out," was the next quick order.

"Oh, God bless us," was all the old man could say as he turned and went inside.

"We want the key," says the fellow in command when the last article of furniture was out. But, God help us, there was no lock to the door. The bar of iron on the inside was never used because the door was always unbarred, and a sod always burned on the hearth for the poor to come in to light their pipes when passing, either day or night.

The old man brought out the bar. He said afterward what he'd like to have done with it was to give the soldier a blow of it. But he didn't. He threw it toward him on the road.

An ejected family

"You damn swine," muttered the soldier. He rode off with his men to the next house.

Before the sun was gone down that evening, every tenant in that townland was homeless. It was a sad picture, my father said, to see two or three little families talking between themselves trying to console each other, and trying to plan some way out of their troubles.

'Twas a sad tale. Not one tenant ever went back to till a sod of land. They scattered everywhere. Three families, two families of the Mahonys and a McCarthy family, went off to America. The money they made off their few cows paid their passage over. I never heard to what part of America they went, for when the old neighbors had scattered away, the emigrants didn't know where to send a line to. So they were never heard of after.

—*Sean Crowley, County Cork*

In the west of Ireland

Emigration and the Ships

Honoured Sir,

Hugh Bohey is a man that has ten in family. The support of them will soon destroy him in these awful times, unless he gets sending some of them to America. He can at least spare three and will send them to America if your honour gives any assistance.

By doing so, they can send me some relief. It will enable me to pay your honour the rent as usual. If you do not assist me, we will in a short time be very desolate and all become paupers.

—Letter from Hugh Bohey to the landlord's agent, County Sligo

One night during the Famine my father remembered two men coming to the house. Each of them had a farm of about ten acres. They asked my grandfather to give them £10 apiece for the two farms—they were going to America. He refused and they pleaded. My grandmother pleaded for them, too. In the end, he gave them £10 apiece for the farms.

—*Hugh Clarke, County Cavan*

Irish emigrants leaving home—the priest's blessing

In company with one a humble priest, I came to a sharp turn in the road. We were in view of the packing of an entire village. There were not more than half a dozen houses on the spot. All their former inmates were preparing to leave. When my reverend friend was recognized, the people gathered about him in the most affectionate manner. He had a word of advice to Pat, a caution to Nelly, a suggestion to Mick. And he made a promise to Dan to take care of the "old woman" until the five pounds came in the spring to his "Reverence" to send her over to America.

Then came tears and lamentation. The priest stood for a while surrounded on bended knees by the old and the young, the strong and the infirm. He turned his moistened eyes toward heaven and asked the blessing of the Almighty upon the wanderers during their long and weary journey. Many were the tears brushed quietly away from the sunburnt cheeks of those who knelt there.

—*James Mulloy, County Cork*

Emigrants leaving Cork—a scene on the quay

The depopulation of this district during the years 1845 to 1855 or so, according to what I can gather, is almost unbelievable. It was caused far more by emigration than by deaths caused by hunger, although hunger took its toll in every district here. I would say that between two-thirds and four-fifths, young and old, disappeared, mainly through starvation, but principally through emigration. The general exodus was to America and Canada after the Famine. Many, many families have disappeared. The ruined houses are proof of that.

The voyage, I was told, took sixteen weeks. Besides their ordinary dress-wearing clothes, each emigrant had to bring bedclothes, a feather tick, blankets, and pillow. . . . Each person brought a supply of oaten cakes baked three times. They were baked in the ordinary way first, then allowed to cool. Then they were baked again until each large cake was hard as a stone.

I was always told that Sligo emigrants left home in secret. They went onboard the ship at the dead of night. I asked, why not go at daytime? They said if the emigrants went in the daytime, and if the landlord knew of their going, he might hold them and take from them money and everything else they had. So their last state would be worse than their first. They would have nothing then at home to live on, and then not be able to emigrate.

—*J. O'Kane, County Sligo*

Old Pat MacQuail told us stories of deaths onboard, and how the body was sown up in canvas and consigned to the deep. He added horrifying details, which may or may not be true: how the sailor who sewed up the corpses stuck his needle into the dead body to oil it so that the point would pass more easily through the canvas. And how a shark always followed the ship when anyone was slipped from a plank over the gunwale into the sea. —*Pilib Ó Conaill, County Meath*

Scene between decks

Military manoeuvres

Those Who Stayed

I remember when you'd see forty boys and girls below there on a Sunday evening, diverting themselves. But now all this country is gone lonesome and bewildered, and there's no man knows what ails it. *—An old man, County Wicklow*

———◆———

I remember that Grandfather would become furious with us when we were young if he saw any of us wasting food. He would refer to the Famine. And when he was ploughing he would not leave a potato however small that the plough would turn up, without picking it up.

There is an account of one Sean óg Mac Cuinneagáin [Cunningham]. In the Famine years and after he never sat down to a meal without going to the door to inspect the road in the hope of finding someone who would have a share of his meal. *—John Cunningham, County Donegal*

Owen Eagan
Mallow, County Cork, Ireland
25th March, 1875

Michael Eagan
Atlanta, Georgia
USA

My Dear Michael,

I trust that your wife and yourself are in the enjoyment of good health. I hope you are far better than I.

I had several attacks of the cold during the winter, so much so that I was obliged to keep to the bed during the greater part of the time, and I am very far from being quite well yet. I lost a good deal to the thatching of my house last winter, and am now at a loss how to draw out my manure and set my garden.

I am sure that I have only to apply to you, and that you will supply me with the means not only of setting my garden, but also of cutting a share of turf for myself.

I made several inquiries about your mother-in-law and am happy to inform you that she is doing very well. If my health permitted, I would be anxious to go see her before I die.

Father Murphy is in good health, though he had a great attack last year. Your sister Mary is a little improved, but her hand is quite lifeless yet. She is keeping two of her children to the school, but she must keep the elder girl at home to do the work of the house, which is a great pity, as she is a nice smart child.

Hoping that you will let me know in your next letter how Pat Sullivan and family are, I remain

Your affectionate Father,
Owen Eagan

Owen Eagen
Mallow, County Cork, Ireland
11th October, 1876

Mrs. Michael Eagan
Atlanta, Georgia
USA

My Dear Mrs. Eagan,

I am very much surprised that you have not written to me ever since the death of my poor son, Michael. I hope however that you and your son are in good health, and that you did not have to leave your house.

My own health, though not at all good for several years, is very bad since the death of my son. It was a shock to me in many ways. As his father it was but quite natural that I should be grieved at his death; and besides, he was my only support in my declining years. But I hope I will not murmur at the will of God.

I hope that you will send me a photograph of the little boy, as I should like to see even his picture before I die. If you see your brother-in-law, Tim Eagan, I hope you will try and induce him to send me something. Or if you do not see him that you would write a feeling letter to him to send something to his father. You can tell him that Father Murphy, the last prop on whom I had to depend, died in March last year, which means I was left utterly destitute.

Hoping that you will not forget to write as soon as you receive this and also that you will send the child's picture, I remain your affectionate father-in-law,

Owen Eagan

Man selling walking sticks

I'm not strong at all, not strong the way I was. If I had two glasses of whiskey I'd dance a hornpipe would dazzle your eyes. But the way I am at this minute you could knock me down with a rush.

I have a noise in my head, so that you wouldn't hear the river at the side of it, and I can't sleep at nights. I do be lying in the darkness thinking of all that was happened in three-score years to the families of Wicklow—what this son did, and what that son did, and of all that went across the sea, and wishing black hell would seize them that never wrote three words to say were they alive or in good health.

That's the profession I have now—to be thinking of all the people, and of the times that's gone.
—*A County Wicklow man*

Patrick Lyons, the author's grandfather

One Who Left

Patrick was born in County Donegal, Ireland, in 1869. Two years later, his parents, Edward and Mary, came to America. Fearing that their son might die on the voyage, they left him behind in the care of Mary's mother.

At age fourteen, Patrick joined his parents in America. He first worked as an errand boy in a general store in Washington, Indiana. Later he became an "Irish peddler," selling fine Irish linens across the country in a wagon pulled by Texas ponies.

Around 1893, Patrick moved to Atlanta, Georgia, where he prospered. He worked for Atlanta Brewery, bought numerous properties for his parents and himself, and married in 1908. Eventually he started his own brewery and at one time he owned the largest saloon in the city. —*Hannah Lyons, Patrick's sister*

A Note to the Reader

I saw my first Famine graveyard in 1992. The country road was narrow, my husband and I were travel-weary, and our rental car seemed to be sealed in a gray envelope of rain. We were anxious to reach the guest house where we would stay that night. Then we noticed the small white sign with black letters. FAMINE GRAVEYARD, it said, with an arrow that pointed left. I remember the sign well. It looked apologetic, as if embarrassed by its own words.

As we turned left and drove deeper into the dripping woods, I wondered what we would find. Neat rows of tombstones, each topped with a Celtic cross? A plaque with names? When we reached the graveyard, we were quiet with sorrow. The graveyard was only a grassy area surrounded by a stone wall. In the middle lay a large flat round stone, probably an old millstone. Nothing else identified this lonely spot as the resting place of starved men, women, and children.

I later learned that the bodies of countless victims of the great hunger lay in similar mass graves. The location of many of these graveyards is still unknown, though some have been identified since the beginning of the 150th anniversary of the Famine in 1995. A cross, plaque, or monument now commemorates the deaths of those buried there. For the nameless dead who are waiting to be found, this book is my tribute.

—*Mary E. Lyons, November 1999*

Famine graveyard, Donegal town, County Donegal, 1999

Acknowledgments

The author is grateful to the following for their patient help:

Moytura Press for permission to quote from *The Rocky Road to Dublin: The Story of a Donegal Man.*

The University of Dublin for permission to reproduce *Discovery of the potato blight in Ireland* on page 17.

Reproduction of the illustrations on pages 10, 11, 12, 13, 16, 18, 19, 20, 33, 34, 38, and 48 courtesy of the National Gallery of Ireland.

The staff of the National Library of Ireland, Dublin, Ireland, including N. Brady, Anita Joyce, G. Kavanagh, Noel Kissane, Sandra McDermott, and J. O'Shea.

The staff at the Department of Irish Folklore, University of Dublin, Dublin, Ireland, including Bairbre Ní Fhloinn, Séamus Ó Catháin, and Críostoir Mac Cárthaigh.

The Trustees of the National Library of Ireland for permission to reproduce the photographs on pages 30 and 41 and the drawings on pages 6, 21 (top), 24, and 28, and the letter from Hugh Boey (NLI Ms 20, 370; O'Hara Papers).

Cathal Póirtéir for his book *Famine Echoes.* His initial transcriptions of Irish Folklore Commission documents made *Feed the Children First* possible.

Charles Young, William Reiss, and Jon Lanman, for their enthusiasm and support.

Marie Moriarity, who made it possible to work on part of this book in Ireland.

Peadar Little for his help with spellings and meanings of Gaelic words.

My second cousin, Ellen Sutter Kappel, for her grandmother's dictated story of Patrick Lyons, and for caring enough to find the Lyons side of the family.

Go raibh maith agat.

The Head of the Department of Irish Folklore, University College, Dublin (IFC) for permission to quote directly from volumes in the Main Manuscript Collection. IFC volume numbers are followed by page numbers.

Page 7, 28: Kate Flood   IFC 1480: 136–37
Pages 13, 16, 18: William Torrens   IFC 1072: 376–400
Page 14: Barney Gargan   IFC 1075: 602–03
Pages 14–15: J. O'Kane   IFC 1072: 241, 242 (paraphrased)

Illustrations Credits

The Twelve Pins, Connemara

Bibliography

Berry, James. *Tales of Old Ireland,* edited by Gertrude Horgan. London: Robinson Publishing, 1984.

Kinealy, Christine. *This Great Calamity: The Irish Famine 1845-52.* Boulder, Colorado: Roberts Rinehart, 1995.

Kissane, Noel. *The Irish Famine: A Documentary History.* Dublin: National Library of Ireland, 1995.

MacManus, Seumus. *The Rocky Road to Dublin: The Story of a Donegal Man,* second edition. Dublin, Moytura Press, 1988.

Moody, T. W., and F. X. Martin, eds. *The Course of Irish History.* Boulder, Colorado: Roberts Rinehart, 1995.

Póirtéir, Cathal. *Famine Echoes.* Dublin: Gill and MacMillan, 1995.

Synge, J. M. *J. M. Synge in Wicklow, West Kerry and Connemara.* Totowa, New Jersey: Rowman and Littlefield, 1980.